D0842599

Shall We Dance?

JAZZ DANCE

by Candice Ransom

FOCUS READERS

www.focusreaders.com

Focus Readers is distributed by North Star Editions:
sales@northstareditions.com | 888-417-0195

Produced for Focus Readers by Red Line Editorial.

Photographs ©: joshblake/iStockphoto, cover, 1; criben/Shutterstock Images, 4–5; erlucho/iStockphoto, 6; Igor Bulgarin/Shutterstock Images, 8, 25; 3bugsmom/iStockphoto, 10–11; Lorraine Swanson/Shutterstock Images, 13, 21; artJazz/iStockphoto, 14–15; Antonio_Diaz/iStockphoto, 17; FatCamera/iStockphoto, 18, 22–23; Charles Sykes/Invision/AP Images, 27; dhorsey/Shutterstock Images, 29

ISBN
978-1-63517-276-8 (hardcover)
978-1-63517-341-3 (paperback)
978-1-63517-471-7 (ebook pdf)
978-1-63517-406-9 (hosted ebook)

Library of Congress Control Number: 2017935126

Printed in the United States of America
Mankato, MN
June, 2017

About the Author

Candice Ransom is the author of 135 books for children. Although she wanted to be a dancer, she became a writer instead. She takes Jazzercise classes, a form of exercise based on jazz dance, and lives in Fredericksburg, Virginia.

TABLE OF CONTENTS

CHAPTER 1

AMERICAN MUSIC, AMERICAN DANCE

The curtain rises. Five dancers are standing still. Then a lively song begins. The dancers step to the side, snapping their fingers. Suddenly they leap into the air.

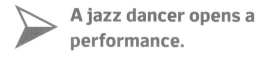

A jazz dancer opens a performance.

 Jazz music brought together new instruments and rhythms.

They land like cats. Their jazz dance is just getting started!

Jazz dance is based on jazz music. This music began around 1900 in New Orleans, Louisiana.

Many people from Europe and West Africa lived there. Each group had its own culture in the United States. Europeans came with instruments such as pianos and trumpets. Africans added **upbeat** rhythms. When combined, a new kind of music was born.

DANCE TIP

Make sure to warm up before a dance class. Jogging in place or jumping jacks are good warm-ups.

 Jazz dancing is common in musicals.

But people did more than just listen to jazz. They also danced to it. They hopped, twisted, and twirled to the peppy music. This led to new dancing styles. These included tap and swing dancing.

At first, these dances were all called jazz dance. That changed in the 1950s. Jazz dance became a smoother style. It also became a performance dance. That's why jazz dance is most often seen in **Broadway** shows and movie musicals. Today's jazz dance uses movements from ballet, tap, and modern dance styles.

CHAPTER 2

CLOTHES MAKE THE DANCE

Jazz dancers wear clothing that lets them move easily. Jazz pants are common. They are stretchy and loose at the ankle. Women often wear a **leotard** and tights. Men might wear a simple T-shirt.

 Jazz dancers often wear matching costumes for performances.

The right shoes are important. Jazz shoes are made of soft leather. It lets the dancer's foot flex. Stiff shoes don't work well. They make it hard to jump. Jazz shoes have a smooth, round patch on the bottom. It lets dancers turn quickly. Some jazz shoes are lace-up style. Others are slip-ons.

DANCE TIP

Some dancers prefer tights. Tights help keep your muscles warm.

On stage, jazz dancers perform in **costumes**. The costumes are fun. Hats and gloves can be used. So can canes. Sparkles and glitter show off the dancers' moves.

CHAPTER 3

STEPPIN' OUT

Jazz dance is a high-energy style. Dancers move their whole bodies. But you can also do **isolations**. For example, hold your arms out. Then shift your hips from side to side.

Dancers can do isolations with their hands, heads, hips, ribs, or shoulders.

Don't move any other body part. This movement isolates your hips.

Isolations are combined with steps. You can step forward with your right foot in a jazz walk. At the same time, your left shoulder moves up. The shoulder isolation adds flair to the movement.

DANCE TIP

Practice doing isolations in front of a mirror. Keep other parts of your body still.

▷ **A dancer practices her jazz moves.**

Certain moves set jazz dance apart from other types of dance. The fingers of a jazz dancer are often spread wide. That is called jazz hands. Fast, little kicks forward are called flick kicks.

 Jazz dancing is great exercise.

A grapevine is a popular step. First, you step to your right. Then your left leg crosses behind your right foot and taps down. **Chassé** is a move borrowed from ballet. You step out to the right. Then you slide your left foot to meet your right foot. This step is performed moving quickly across the floor.

Turning, jumping, and leaping are harder moves. They make jazz dance exciting to watch.

DANCE TIP

Take time after class to stretch your muscles. Stretching helps prevent injury.

JAZZ SQUARE

This four-step move follows the shape of a square. Start with your feet together.

1. Bring your right foot across your left foot. Your legs will be crossed.
2. Next, step back with your left foot. Your weight will be on your left foot.
3. Step your right leg out to the right side.
4. Finally, swing your left foot in front of your right foot. Now you're ready to do another jazz square!

A young dancer does a jazz square.

CHAPTER 4

SHOWTIME!

Jazz dancers take classes. They spend many hours practicing. Young dancers train at local **studios**. Serious dancers move on to bigger studios. Studios often compete against each other.

Becoming a star takes a lot of practice.

The best dancers even perform in professional shows.

To get a job in a show, dancers **audition**. Many dancers might try out for the same job. They give a short performance for the people running the show. If a dancer passes the audition, he or she is hired.

Many dancers want to be in a Broadway show. But there are other jobs for dancers.

 Many jazz dancers yearn to perform in shows.

Dancers can work on a cruise ship. Cruise ships are large boats. People take trips on them for vacation. The ships often provide entertainment for the passengers.

Dancers **rehearse** most days and perform in live shows. They also get to visit new places.

Theme parks also need dancers. A cast of dancers will put on shows every day. Other jobs include dancing in movies, TV commercials,

DANCE TIP

If you can, take a dance class in a different style, along with jazz dance lessons. Successful jazz dancers take classes in ballet, modern dance, and hip-hop.

 Jazz dancers perform at the Tony Awards.

and music videos. Many dancers tour with singers or bands. Jazz dancers also compete on TV talent shows.

FOCUS ON
JAZZ DANCE

Write your answers on a separate piece of paper.

1. Suppose you went shopping for clothes and shoes for your first jazz class. Write a letter to your friend describing what you bought.

2. Would you rather dance in a Broadway show or on a cruise ship? Why?

3. Which move is borrowed from ballet?
    A. grapevine
    B. flick kick
    C. chassé

4. How did people from West Africa help create jazz music?
    A. with their singing
    B. with their dancing
    C. with their rhythms

5. What does **high-energy** mean in this book?
   *Jazz dance is a **high-energy** style. Dancers move their whole bodies.*
   - **A.** with lots of effort and movement
   - **B.** with lots of teamwork
   - **C.** with lots of time and space

6. What does the word **flex** mean in this book?
   *Jazz shoes are made of soft leather. It lets the dancer's foot **flex**.*
   - **A.** to stay protected
   - **B.** to cool down
   - **C.** to move freely

Answer key on page 32.

GLOSSARY

audition
To give a short performance as a test.

Broadway
An area in New York City where there are many theaters.

chassé
A step where one foot moves and the other foot meets it.

costumes
Special outfits to wear onstage.

isolations
Movements that separate one part of the body from the others.

leotard
A formfitting one-piece garment that dancers wear.

rehearse
To practice for a public performance.

studios
Rooms or buildings where dancers practice.

upbeat
Happy or cheerful.

TO LEARN MORE

BOOKS

Fuhrer, Margaret. *American Dance: The Complete Illustrated History*. Minneapolis: Voyageur Press, 2014.

Robey, James. *Beginning Jazz Dance*. Champaign, IL: Human Kinetics, 2016.

Tieck, Sarah. *Dancing*. Minneapolis: ABDO, 2013.

NOTE TO EDUCATORS

Visit **www.focusreaders.com** to find lesson plans, activities, links, and other resources related to this title.

INDEX

Answer Key: 1. Answers will vary; **2.** Answers will vary; **3.** C; **4.** C; **5.** A; **6.** C